# Blueprints for Life

## 25 Devotions for Living by God's Design

**Tim Wesemann**

www.CTAinc.com

*Blueprints for Life*
*25 Devotions for Living by God's Design*
by Tim Wesemann
www.timwesemann.com

Copyright © 2006 by CTA, Inc.
1625 Larkin Williams Rd.
Fenton, MO 63026-1205

Unless otherwise indicated, all Scripture is taken from the HOLY BIBLE, NEW INTERNATIONAL VERSION®. Copyright © 1973, 1978, 1984 International Bible Society. Used by permission of Zondervan. All rights reserved.

Scripture quotations marked ESV are taken from The Holy Bible, English Standard Version, copyright © 2001 by Crossway Bibles, a division of Good News Publishers. Used by permission. All rights reserved.

Scripture quotations from THE MESSAGE are copyright © by Eugene H. Peterson 1993, 1994, 1995, 1996, 2000, 2001, 2002. Used by permission of NavPress Publishing Group.

The Scripture quotations marked "NKJV" are taken from the New King James Version. Copyright © 1982 by Thomas Nelson, Inc. Used by permission. All rights reserved.

The Scripture quotation marked NLT is taken from the Holy Bible, New Living Translation, copyright © 1996. Used by permission of Tyndale House Publishers, Inc., Wheaton, Illinois 60189. All rights reserved.

ISBN 1-933234-05-9
Printed in Thailand

# Surveying God's Plan

*God picked you out as his from the very start.*
*Think of it:*
*included in God's original plan of salvation*
*by the bond of faith in the living truth.*
*This is the life of the Spirit*
*he invited you to*
*through the Message we delivered,*
*in which you get in on the glory*
*of our Master, Jesus Christ.*

2 Thessalonians 2:13–14 THE MESSAGE

# Day 1

## The Design Plan
### Scriptural Foundation: Ephesians 1:3–8

Consider this, if you can:
- before running water,
- before the sun rose,
- before anyone could go out on a limb,
- before mountains and molehills,
- before creating began . . .

we were on God's mind. In fact, we were more than on his mind; we were in his heart. The divine architect included each of us in a prominent place in the design of his plan of creation and salvation. That's almost unfathomable, isn't it?

Ephesians 1:3–8 confirms those facts! Paul, under the inspiration of the Holy Spirit, tells God's people that the Father

- blessed us with "every spiritual blessing in Christ";
- chose us in Christ "before the creation of the world to be holy and blameless in his sight";
- adopted us as his children according to "his pleasure and will";
- planned to provide redemption for us through Jesus' blood;
- forgave our sins by grace, through the sacrifice of Jesus; and
- lavished us "with all wisdom and understanding."

What a firm foundation of salvation our Father has constructed for our lives in Christ Jesus! We aren't some quick afterthought. He did not clumsily cobble onto his original design. No. Even before the creation of the world, God the Father poured and firmly bonded our salvation through Jesus Christ, our Savior.

No matter how good a design for life is, it's doomed to fail if it's not based on Jesus Christ. For the next five weeks we'll explore foundational living: What does it mean to build our lives firmly on the foundation of Jesus Christ? How can we step down from the shaky pedestals on which we often teeter? Borrowing from the images and terminology of architecture and construction, these devotional readings drawn from the Holy Scriptures will lead us to live more firmly and joyfully on the only secure foundation—Christ Jesus our Lord.

Praise be to the God and Father of our Lord Jesus Christ, who has blessed us in the heavenly realms with every spiritual blessing in Christ.

Ephesians 1:3

*Prayer suggestion:* Father, our minds can't comprehend the fact that you chose us before the creation of the world to live free and secure, anchored in Christ himself. Through these devotions, help us to trust more firmly the wonders of your love, love we do not yet fully understand. In the name of Jesus we pray and live. Amen.

# Day 2

### The Houses
Scriptural Foundation: 2 Corinthians 5:1

Tent-camping never appealed much to me. I never seem to rest comfortably in tents. They don't give the protection I'd like when major storms blow up. (Or when predator animals of major size appear!) Tents seem to come in one of two temperatures—hot or cold. No, give me a sturdy brick house, indoor plumbing, and a thermostat. I'm much happier with at least minimal modern conveniences!

When it comes to life in tents, God shares my attitude:

> *Now we know that if the earthly tent we live in is destroyed, we have a building from God, an eternal house in heaven, not built by human hands.*
>
> 2 Corinthians 5:1

In these words the apostle Paul compares our earthly, physical bodies to tents and points out their limitations. Our lives in these earthly bodies will never be completely comfortable. They are

- temporary,
- often unsafe,
- frequently uncomfortable, and
- ultimately destructible.

In the beginning, God created perfect people with perfect bodies, wonderful bodies! But Adam's first sin opened the door on Planet Earth to aches and pains, surgeries and therapy, vitamins and supplements, heating pads and ice packs, death and grief, and so much more. Now perfect comfort will come only in the perfection of our heavenly home!

Tent dwellers take note: your situation is only temporary. In death we will give up our tentlike bodies. In heaven we will inherit a permanent home from God. Human hands didn't construct our indestructible heavenly home, but our Savior's outstretched hands nailed to the cross made it possible for us to one day live there.

*Now we know that if the earthly tent we live in is destroyed, we have a building from God, an eternal house in heaven, not built by human hands.*

2 Corinthians 5:1

*Prayer suggestion:* Thank you, gracious Father, for my home here on earth and the heavenly home Jesus is preparing for me. Thank you for the earthly "tent" of my body and for the glorified body you will one day give me in your presence. May I serve as a faithful steward of my temporary tent until, by your grace and Christ's sacrifice, I live forever glorified in my permanent home in heaven. In Jesus' name. Amen.

# Day 3

## The Cross Streets
Scriptural Foundation: Acts 2:22–24

According to a 1993 Census Bureau publication, the most common street name isn't First Street, it's Second! Third is second and First is third. In case you're wondering, Fourth came in fourth while Park beat out Fifth for fifth place! Confused yet?

Consider the streets that intersect closest to your home. Now consider your life itself as a house or home. Since you are built on the foundation of Jesus Christ, what names do you expect to find on the crossroads at the corner of your life? Might we say that you reside at the corner of Grace and Resurrection Streets? If so, you live in a great neighborhood, surrounded on every side by God's gifts!

As Peter preached to his fellow Jews after the Holy Spirit filled their lives on the day of Pentecost (Acts 2), his excitement for living life built on the foundation of Jesus Christ overflowed. He spoke from a heart filled with urgency that everyone move into this neighborhood, the world's only safe neighborhood.

Peter told his listeners about Jesus' horrific death, a death that took place where Grace and Resurrection Streets intersect. Their sins (and yours and mine!) made that death necessary. Yet by that death, Jesus turned a dead-end street into a bustling, living, growing neighborhood!

Welcome to Grace Street! Here Jesus offers new life to all who believe. Welcome to Grace Street! Jesus took the punishment we deserved upon himself and has given us in exchange full and free forgiveness. Welcome to Grace Street!

But the story Peter told his hearers that day did not end with Jesus' crucifixion. God raised Jesus from the dead. Welcome to Resurrection Street! In Jesus, we know for certain we will one day rise from death to live, personally and individually, with Jesus forever. Welcome to Resurrection Street! Living out our Spirit-created faith, we rise each new day to brand new life. Welcome to Resurrection Street!

So what streets intersect closest to where you live? Ahhh, that's what I thought . . . you live on the foundation of Jesus Christ—at the corner of Grace and Resurrection Streets.

> But God raised him from the dead, freeing him from the agony of death, because it was impossible for death to keep its hold on him.
>
> Acts 2:24

*Prayer suggestion:* Your grace overwhelms me, my Savior. Your death and resurrection for my salvation have changed me forever! For now and forever, keep me living close to you at the corner of Grace and Resurrection Streets. Amen.

# Day 4

## The Investment
### Scriptural Foundation: 1 Peter 1:18–21

If you've invested in building or buying a home, you have taken a leap of faith and, if you're like most people, made great sacrifices. As you invested so much of yourself—your time, your energy, and your money—in the project, did your emotions run the gamut from excitement to cautious concern to downright panic? Was the house the right one? Would the investment pay off? Over time, would the property values rise—or fall?

Now try to grasp the enormity of the investment God made so that you and I would have the opportunity to live on the firm foundation of Jesus Christ. We're used to thinking about investments in terms of money, stocks, bonds, or real estate. But none of these kinds of investments, no matter how great their worth, can compare with what God poured into the enterprise of saving us from sin, death, and the devil.

Meditate on this truth from 1 Peter 1:18–21:

> For you know that it was not with perishable things such as silver or gold that you were redeemed from the empty way of life handed down to you from your forefathers, but with the precious blood of Christ, a lamb without blemish or defect. He was chosen before the creation of the world, but was revealed in these last times for your sake. Through him you believe in God, who raised him from the dead and glorified him, and so your faith and hope are in God.

Our ransom cost Jesus his life. He poured out his life's blood to purchase us, to buy us back from the slavery into which we by our sin had sold ourselves. Christ became the perfect sacrifice for our sins.

As we consider investing our money, many of us spend weeks, months, even years searching out the specific instruments that will earn the highest returns. Whenever we invest our time, energy, or talents, we usually expect maximum return on those investments. Our time is precious, our resources limited, and our energies often sapped. Jesus went all the way to the cross and the garden tomb for us. He invested his very life so we could live!

Now how do we respond to such an investment, for heaven's sake?

And so your faith and hope are in God.

1 Peter 1:21

*Prayer suggestion:* Lord Jesus, in response to your investment in my salvation, I want to return my whole life to you. I will thank and praise you eternally for all you have done for me! Amen.

# Day 5

### Title Deed
Scriptural Foundation: 2 Corinthians 1:21–22

When a family builds its own home, family members often enjoy etching their names in the fresh concrete of the foundation. The etching carries no official weight, but it's fun anyway! It marks the house and property as belonging to that family. It tells all future owners who lived there first.

Most of us like being able to say, "I own this" or "I paid for this myself—you'll never guess how much it cost!" or "I worked hard for this—it's mine." Even when we receive a gift, we may boast, "This is mine now." We hold on to our possessions as if we will never let them go.

The apostle Paul used this common experience when he wrote:

> Now it is God who makes both us and you stand firm in Christ. He anointed us, set his seal of ownership on us, and put his Spirit in our hearts as a deposit, guaranteeing what is to come.
>
> 2 Corinthians 1:21–22

Christ has set his mark upon us, put his Spirit in us. We belong to him! It may seem nearly impossible to believe, but we bring him great joy. Using his divine finger, our creating, saving God etched this into our lives: "This one belongs to me. In my Son, Jesus, I have adopted this person, rescued him or her from sin and death."

Since we ourselves belong to him, it naturally follows that all the material things around us also belong to him. They come to us as his gifts, gifts he lets us use, assets he has chosen to entrust to our care. When someone entrusts something to our care, we do not own it. Yet we certainly intend to care for it. We do not carelessly lose it. We'd want to return it in better condition than when we first received it.

Would it help us as caretakers to plug the phrase "he has entrusted to my care" into our everyday conversation? For instance, I could speak of the faith "he has entrusted to my care"; the Word of grace and truth "he has entrusted to my care"; and the relationships, money, and time "he has entrusted to my care." Each time I mention any of those blessings God has placed in my life, I would remember his kind generosity.

He . . . put his Spirit in our hearts as a deposit, guaranteeing what is to come.

2 Corinthians 1:21–22

*Prayer suggestion:* Gracious and giving Lord, thank you for claiming me and marking me as one of your own. What a humble honor it is to live as your child! You have entrusted so much to my care; make me a faithful caretaker of your gifts. Hear my prayer for Jesus' sake. Amen.

# Days 6-7

## Time for Reflection
### Surveying His Plan

*Over the next two days, reflect on the message of this hymn. Shape your prayers around the words as you think back on the meaning of this week's devotions.*

When I survey the wondrous cross
On which the prince of glory died,
My richest gain I count but loss
And pour contempt on all my pride.

Forbid it, Lord, that I should boast
Save in the death of Christ, my God;
All the vain things that charm me most,
I sacrifice them to his blood.

See, from his head, his hands, his feet
Sorrow and love flow mingled down.
Did e'er such love and sorrow meet
Or thorns compose so rich a crown?

Were the whole realm of nature mine,
That were a tribute far too small;
Love so amazing, so divine,
Demands my soul, my life, my all!

Isaac Watts, 1674–1748

# Blueprints for Life

*You are God's house.*
*Using the gift God gave me*
*as a good architect,*
*I designed blueprints;*
*Apollos is putting up the walls.*

*Let each carpenter*
*who comes on the job*
*take care to build on the foundation!*
*Remember, there is only one foundation,*
*the one already laid:*
*Jesus Christ.*

1 Corinthians 3:9–11 THE MESSAGE

15

# Day 8

*The Basics*
Scriptural Foundation: 1 Corinthians 3:9–11

Take another look. Go ahead. I'll wait as you reread the words from 1 Corinthians on page 15. This text lays out the basics of foundational living. Under the inspiration of the Holy Spirit, Paul chose this picture-story to teach the people the importance of building upon the sure foundation of Jesus Christ rather than on any of the human beings God has chosen to use as construction workers in his building project. Here's what Paul points out:

- God has a master plan for building a temple, a house; each believer is a building block in that house.

- God himself poured the foundation, after poring at length over the plans for the project. At just the right time God sacrificed his Son so that all who believe in Jesus could be forgiven and live forever with him.

- In his infinite wisdom God decided to contract out, if you will, some of the work of building on the foundation. He chose Paul and other apostles as architects; together they designed a plan for making the house larger and more glorious than we can imagine.

- God then chose a variety of subcontractors to rough in the house, gifting each for their tasks. Some, like Apollos and Timothy, preached and taught; others, like Barnabas and Silas, supported these ministries.

- Still today God continues to invite subcontractors onto the work site; gifted in various ways, these workers build on the foundation of Christ, using a variety of God-given gifts.

- Even now in your city, town, or village, the church needs subcontractors to do a variety of tasks: preaching, teaching, ministering to the sick, encouraging, leading children and youth, supporting his work in a host of ways. How important are these tasks! Yet everyone the Lord brings in to work on the project can be sure they stand on firm footing—not on their own skills, but on the sure foundation of Jesus Christ and his saving, sacrificial love.

No one can lay any other foundation than the one we already have—Jesus Christ.

1 Corinthians 3:11 NLT

**Prayer suggestion:** Ask God's blessing upon all his worker-servants. Ask that they always work to God's glory and never their own. Thank him for the variety of gifts he has given to you and those serving around you. And pray for abundant expansion in God's house as we work together to his glory.

# Day 9

## A Firm Foundation
### Scriptural Foundation: Isaiah 33:6

These words from Isaiah 33:6 (ESV) paint an exquisite picture:

> *. . . he will be the stability of your times.*

Stability? Yes, stability. We may use other words to describe it, words such as *security* or *dependability* or *permanence,* but in one form or another we all long for stability. Compared with many people around the world, we in North America do enjoy considerable stability. Still, we cannot with 100 percent assurance predict what might happen today in our homes, workplaces, or schools.

At any moment, great news could come running through the front door of our lives. Or tragedy might sneak in through the back door when we least expect it.

Stability? At best, it's a dream while we live here on earth. Yet as Christians we find help, hope, and comfort in knowing that our Savior brings stability. He is the sure, firm foundation on which we build:

> *The word of the Lord stands forever.* 1 Peter 1:25

> *His steadfast love endures forever.* Psalm 136 ESV

> *I will never leave you nor forsake you.* Hebrews 13:5 ESV

Jesus was born in a *stable* environment during unstable times in order to bring us stability in our unstable times. Every aspect of his life—his birth, his death, his resurrection, his ascension—brings stability to our lives by securing for us an unshakable relationship and an eternal home with our God.

That's incredible news when so many things we foolishly trust—our money, power, influence, intellect, or position—rest on shifting, unstable sand. Jesus is the only sure foundation on which we build our lives of faith every single day!

*He will be the stability of your times.*

Isaiah 33:6 ESV

***Prayer suggestion:*** Lord, in the presence of others I may act as if everything is wonderful. I may even tell myself that the instability in my life causes me no worry or fear. You know better. You know me better than I know myself. Forgive me, Savior, for relying on these false gods, and place my trust firmly on the foundational truth of Jesus' death for me. I so need the stability that brings! In his name. Amen.

# Day 10

### The Floor Plan
#### Scriptural Foundation: Ezekiel 43:10–11

One night some friends, excited about the plans they had drawn up for building their new house, laid out big pages of blueprints for me to study. It was fascinating and futile at the same time. I got a general idea of how things would look in their new home, but I have never been especially adept at visualizing three-dimensional structures after looking at flat drawings.

Four hundred and eighty years after God rescued the Israelites from slavery in Egypt, Solomon began building a temple of the Lord. Before construction began, the Lord laid out detailed, precise plans for the project (1 Kings 6). How excited Solomon, his people, and the Lord himself must have been as they began to build!

Still today, we serve a God who loves to share his detailed, precise blueprint for foundational living with his people. He wants not a single one of us living haphazardly or thoughtlessly.

And yet we do live that way at times, don't we? Aren't we often indifferent to or careless in our efforts to understand what God himself has in mind for us? If we take a sweeping glance at Scripture's blueprints for Christian living, we might not even see some of our errors in executing the plans the Holy Spirit has detailed for our lives. But if we check in every corner, we soon spot trouble. We see the crookedness we have tolerated, the shallowness of our love, the haphazardness of our obedience. When we see these defects, we have only one refuge. We run to the words of truth written in Christ's blood over the doorposts of our lives:

*If we claim to be without sin, we deceive ourselves and the truth is not in us. If we confess our sins, he is faithful and just and will forgive us our sins and purify us from all unrighteousness.*

1 John 1:8–9

Take another look at God's blueprint for his church. Behold the splendor he intends as his people faithfully study and keep his Word, praise him together in worship, communicate with him in prayer, and support each other in a love that reflects God's own unconditional love for us.

Make known to them the design of the temple.

Ezekiel 43:11

***Prayer suggestion:*** Thank you, Lord, for including me in the house you're building. Thank you for the blueprints in Scripture that provide clear and specific directions for building a life that honors you. Forgive my many failures to perfectly execute those plans, and work your will in me more and more. In Jesus' name. Amen.

# Day 11

The Electrical Layout
Scriptural Foundation: Colossians 1:28–29

Today as I write I feel completely zapped of all energy. My throat hurts, my entire head feels clogged up, my temperature is rising, and my cough is annoying! Frankly, I'm tempted to take my second nap of the day. Oh, don't feel sorry for me—my wife certainly doesn't, so why should you?! Despite my energy level, or lack of it, I sit here writing this devotion.

Okay, okay, I admit that the deadline serves as partial motivation. But much more important, I know that Jesus Christ has chosen me to proclaim his name today. I trust that whatever I write, it will make a difference in someone's life. Not because of my words or insights, but because his unseen energy powerfully works within me. Anything that honors God flows from his energy at work in us, his Spirit living within us and animating our efforts.

Paul wrote to the Colossians:

> *Him we proclaim, warning everyone and teaching everyone with all wisdom, that we may present everyone mature in Christ. For this I toil, struggling with all his energy that he powerfully works within me.*
>
> Colossians 1:28–29 ESV

I like to think of this in terms of the energy wired into a house. We flip a switch and lights shine, computer screens glow, power saws run. We usually don't think about the unseen energy source unless we experience a power outage. Then our world comes to a screeching halt!

Similarly, we often overlook God's energy, the energy that empowers our lives of faith. We so often take credit for ourselves. We so often forget to thank him for working in us and through us. Still, he continues to energize our words and actions. He makes it possible for the light of Christlike love to shine through us, especially as others witness that light in us.

Instead of taking these gifts for granted, let's stop and thank our God for his work in us. Let's thank our Savior for paying our "energy bill" in full, living freely within us and shining through us, so that together with him, we can light up our dark world with his saving Good News—the news of new life in his cross.

*We proclaim him.*

Colossians 1:28

***Prayer suggestion:*** Dear Father, source of all our energy, we praise and thank you for working within us, enabling us to proclaim you as Lord and work with you to present people mature in Christ. Create limitless energy within us for this task, and fill us with your presence and peace. Amen.

# Day 12

The Plot Layout
Scriptural Foundation: Psalm 16:5–6

God has blessed my family with a beautiful, large plot of land on which to live. Trees, bushes, and flowers—some living, some in various stages of dying—line its boundaries. It offers not only pleasant areas in which to play and rest, but also areas that await quite a bit of work. A garage sits on it, but garbage also sits *in* that garage. My lot has it all—the good, the bad, and the downright ugly.

As I consider another plot that God has given me, I see areas of beauty along with areas of failure and sin. I notice the boundary lines. Through them God brought me to faith. I've broken those boundaries many times as I walked away from his will. Later he brought me back to himself again. Forgiveness follows my failures. Do you get the picture? The boundary lines in my life and in yours fall in delightful places. Those lines form the shape of a cross— Christ's cross.

God graciously blesses each of our lives with a lot (in more ways than one). He makes those blessings obvious when we keep our eyes on the green hill far away where our dear Lord died to save us all.

David gives us a lot to consider in Psalm 16:5–6 ESV:

> *The LORD is my chosen portion and my cup; you hold my lot. The lines have fallen for me in pleasant places; indeed, I have a beautiful inheritance.*

A beautiful inheritance indeed! Christ's life, death, and resurrection secured for us a legacy of forgiveness and foreverness, power and peace, joy and contentment, purpose and pleasure, compassion and companionship.

Thinking about the lot with which we've been blessed gives us a lot to consider. Let's consider not only the lot on which we live, but also the lot that houses the Giver of life! The Lord leads us into the greenest of pastures and provides for us an eternal inheritance that cannot fade or rust, an inheritance that no thief can steal. Yes, we have a lot to work on, but we also have a lot to be thankful for!

Indeed, I have a beautiful inheritance.

Psalm 16:6 ESV

***Prayer suggestion:*** Father, the lines of your grace have no limits—they extend to all the world and to all its people. Your forgiveness and salvation have been offered to all. As I consider the boundary lines of my life, I thank you for the rich inheritance with which you have blessed me. My gratitude is eternal. Amen.

# Days 13–14

## Time for Reflection

### Blueprints for Life

*Over the next two days, reflect on the message of this hymn. Shape your prayers around the words as you think back on the meaning of this week's devotions.*

Christ is our cornerstone,
On him alone we build;
With his true saints alone
The courts of heav'n are filled.
On his great love Our hopes we place
Of present grace And joys above.

Oh, then, with hymns of praise
These hallowed courts shall ring;
Our voices we will raise
The Three in One to sing
And thus proclaim In joyful song,
Both loud and long, That glorious name.

Here may we gain from heav'n
The grace which we implore,
And may that grace, once giv'n,
Be with us evermore
Until that day When all the blest
To endless rest Are called away.

Author unknown, Latin, 700
tr. John Chandler, 1806–76

# The Construction Site

*Commit to the LORD whatever you do,*
*and your plans will succeed. . . .*
*In his heart a man plans his course,*
*but the LORD determines his steps.*

Proverbs 16:3–9

# Day 15

### The Construction Site
#### Scriptural Foundation: Genesis 11:1-9

I recall taking a Sunday school field trip to a construction site called Babel. The Flannelgraph Travel Agency took us there. What an amazing trip!

As the Genesis story unfolded in those flannel figures, we learned about people who organized themselves (without inviting God) in Babel to build a city. Their plan for that city included a tower that reached to the heavens. Their project committee made two major mistakes. First, they tried to build their city by themselves, for themselves. And second, they wanted the glory, the power, and the name for themselves.

But God intervened in their selfish plans. He came down and confused their language so the construction workers could not understand one another. Unless the builders communicate, they cannot construct a beautiful, sturdy, and safe structure. So the building at Babel came to a halt.

Today the Holy Spirit builds faithful followers upon the sure foundation of Jesus Christ. Satan watches, desperate to halt the construction's progress. Whereas God used language confusion to remind his people to communicate with him, Satan uses it to cause hurt and misunderstanding among us. Oftentimes Satan plugs our ears (our most important tool for communication) to keep us from listening to each other. He tries his best to sever our communication lines with God, too, tempting our hearts to focus on ourselves rather than on Christ Jesus.

Satan skillfully manipulates his tools. He hammers bitterness into our hearts. He leaves vices lying around to tempt us. He attempts to saw solid relationships into pieces. He uses a fake level to give the false impression of a healthy balance in our lives. He whittles down our relationships with jealousy, out-of-control anger, spite, and vengeance. He nails us with words that hurt.

How thankful we can be, though, that the plans of our architect, Jesus Christ, overpower those of Satan. He communicated this to us perfectly at another site, a site where Roman nails pinned our Savior to the cross. There Jesus communicated reconciliation. At that construction site, Jesus built relationships like no others, eternal and holy relationships.

Then they said, "Come, let us build ourselves a city."

Genesis 11:4

*Prayer suggestion:* Father, using two pieces of wood (in the shape of a cross), rebuild my life. Set it firmly upon the sure foundation of my forgiving Savior, Jesus Christ. In his name I pray and live. Amen.

# Day 16

The Workers
Scriptural Foundation: Romans 12:6–13

Foundational Living, Inc.

*Job Description*

Title: Construction worker

Primary Responsibility: Building God's kingdom on the sure
foundation of Jesus Christ

Supervision: You will report directly to God the Father, in Jesus'
name.

Previous Experience Necessary: None. Each worker receives
one-on-one, on-the-job training from God the Holy Spirit.

Qualifications:
- Spirit-created faith that loves the Lord
- Willingness to use God-given gifts
- Willingness to learn from Jesus to rejoice with others
  and hurt with those who suffer

Responsibilities:
- Serving as the Spirit guides
- Giving to God daily the glory and praise
- Hating what is evil, and clinging to what is good
- Being joyful in hope, patient in affliction, faithful in
  prayer
- Practicing hospitality
- Forgiving as you have been forgiven in Christ's cross

Opportunities for Growth:
- Strength, through the study of God's Word
- Forgiveness, through Jesus' redemptive work
- Satisfaction, through work with God's people
- Comfort, through shared encouragement

*We have different gifts, according to the grace given us.*

Romans 12:6

***Prayer suggestion:*** Thank the Lord for the gifts he entrusts to your care and for the opportunities for kingdom-building he has placed around you.

# Day 17

### The Tools
Scriptural Foundation: Galatians 5:22–25

O pen the drawer marked *Galatians 5:22–25* in the tool chest of your Bible, and you'll find nine important tools you need for foundational living in Jesus Christ. The Holy Spirit has provided you with each one. How have you used them in your foundational living?

*Love*—This simple-looking clamp defies logic as it holds relationships together, adheres the heart of Jesus with the hearts of his children, and causes a perfect God to stick with sinful disciples in grace-filled forgiveness.

*Joy*—A great cutting tool that leaves fear, despair, and sadness lying in shreds, ready for disposal.

*Peace*—When guilt, stress, and worry fasten deep under your skin, heaven's tool of peace loosens them like no other tool on earth. Peace releases the tense, unwinds the worriers, and unbinds the guilty.

*Patience*—This tool tightens trusting relationships. Make sure you don't settle for one of the imitation knockoffs. God's model is the best available. This tool will stick it out over the long haul.

*Kindness*—Smooths rough edges that keep people in God's family apart. Keep this tool handy for frequent use!

*Goodness*—If you find yourself connected to unwanted, discarded, or substandard materials, goodness places a wedge between you and the materials, prying them away and restoring the finished product to perfection.

*Faithfulness*—No more unsteady walkways. Faithfulness permanently seals all seams against cracks and separations.

*Gentleness*—This tool easily bores holes through hardened hearts, bitter lives, and stubborn ways.

*Self-control*—This tool calmly levels rough surfaces and makes them ready for use in kingdom-building.

Since we live by the Spirit, let us keep in step with the Spirit.

Galatians 5:25

*Prayer suggestion:* Construct a prayer asking God to strengthen in you the fruit of the Holy Spirit listed above.

# Day 18

## The Heavy Equipment Shed
### Scriptural Foundation: 2 Timothy 3:16–17

Visit any large construction site and you'll see your share of heavy equipment—skid steer loaders, bulldozers, cement mixers, and even cranes. So what heavy equipment does God use at the site where he builds his house? The Bible.

This heavy-duty equipment serves many purposes on the construction site. The apostle Paul outlines these:

> *All Scripture is God-breathed and is useful for teaching, rebuking, correcting and training in righteousness, so that the man of God may be thoroughly equipped for every good work.*
> 2 Timothy 3:16–17

The Bible not only comes from God; its every word is God-breathed. Talk about a piece of multipurpose equipment! Note the variety of tasks it does and purposes it serves:

*Teaching*—God's inspired Word serves as a piece of teaching equipment, instructing us in foundational living. It teaches us that

- God created the heavens and the earth (Genesis 1:1–2:25).
- Jesus is the only way to heaven (John 14:1–6).
- Salvation is the free gift of God's grace (Ephesians 2:8–9).
- Jesus rose from the dead so that one day we, too, will rise (1 Corinthians 15).

*Rebuking*—God's Law shows us in what exact ways we fail to measure up to God's expectations and how much we need the forgiveness and salvation he offers us through Jesus and his cross (Romans 3:23; 6:23; 1 John 1:8–10).

*Correcting*—God's Word levels the ground, not only showing us our sin and how helpless we are to help ourselves, but also leading us down the correct path as the forgiven children of a gracious Father (Psalm 1:1–3; Psalm 119:105).

*Training in Righteousness*—God's Word builds us up in our faith as we, in turn, serve as workers in God's kingdom. Christ's Word, his love, and his sacrifice for us bring out in us a whole new way of living (Galatians 2:20; 2 Corinthians 5:17).

So that the man of God may be thoroughly equipped for every good work.

2 Timothy 3:17

*Prayer suggestion:* Father, keep on using your Word to shape and form me as I grow up on the foundation of Jesus Christ. Teach, rebuke, correct, and train me in righteousness. In your name I pray this. Amen.

# Day 19

Hard Hat Area
Scriptural Foundation: Ephesians 4:14–16

*Hard Hat Area!* Whenever I see that warning sign, instinct leads me to look up! I realize that it's not the smartest thing to do on an active construction site. But I do it anyway. I want to take a look at what's being built (or destroyed) above me.

Here's a little hard hat trivia:

- Hard hats first appeared on the scene in the late 1800s. The San Francisco Golden Gate Bridge construction site became America's first designated hard hat area.
- Falling rivets could cause serious injury, and so the Bullard Company transformed a mining helmet into an industrial hard hat for the construction site.
- The steel used to make the first hard hats came from Bethlehem, Pennsylvania.
- Over the years, hard hats have undergone many changes, but their purpose remains the same—personal protection.

Just prior to denoting Jesus as the head of his body, the church, in Ephesians 4, Paul the apostle warns that with so many ideas about Jesus, salvation, and God's grace floating around in the world, any of us could easily be hit by uncertainty or fall prey to deceit. In essence, we live in a hard hat area!

But in this hard hat area, it's okay to look up! In fact, the Holy Spirit encourages us to do just that—to look up and praise the forgiving Christ, who is the sure foundation on which we live.

This Jesus also came from Bethlehem—not Bethlehem, Pennsylvania, but the little town in Palestine on the other side of the world where Christ and Christmas were born! Jesus came to be our world's Savior. He came to serve and protect his people. That purpose will not change so long as we live in this world, a world filled with dangerous temptations and the fears and doubts that threaten to seriously damage our faith. Yesterday. Today. Forever. Jesus provides effective personal protection for us, his body, the church he so loves!

*We will in all things grow up into him who is the Head, that is, Christ.*
Ephesians 4:15

*Prayer suggestion:* Protect my faith, my heart, my life, Jesus, or I will die. Never let me compromise the truth of your Word. Give me courage to stand up for your truth in a world of lies and partial truths. You are the foundation on which I live and build. Amen.

# Days 20–21

Time for Reflection

### The Construction Site

*Over the next two days, reflect on the message of this hymn. Shape your prayers around the words as you think back on the meaning of this week's devotions.*

Rock of Ages, cleft for me,
Let me hide myself in thee;
Let the water and the blood,
From thy riven side which flowed,
Be of sin the double cure:
Cleanse me from its guilt and pow'r.

Nothing in my hand I bring;
Simply to thy cross I cling.
Naked, come to thee for dress;
Helpless, look to thee for grace;
Foul, I to the fountain fly;
Wash me, Savior, or I die.

While I draw this fleeting breath,
When mine eyelids close in death,
When I soar to worlds unknown,
See thee on thy judgment throne,
Rock of Ages, cleft for me,
Let me hide myself in thee.

Augustus M. Toplady, 1740–78

# Foundation Components

Then I said to them,
"You see the trouble we are in. . . .
Come, let us rebuild the wall of Jerusalem,
and we will no longer be in disgrace."
I also told them about the gracious hand
of my God upon me and
what the king had said to me.
They replied,
"Let us start rebuilding."
So they began this good work.

Nehemiah 2:17–18

# Day 22

## Sill Plate and Tie Bolts
### Scriptural Foundation: Nehemiah 1:1–2:20

For the next few days we will watch our Scripture readings unfold from the book of Nehemiah. In this book we read the story of the rebuilding of Jerusalem's city wall—in an astonishingly short fifty-two days! The Scripture readings I will suggest for your meditation each day are longer; most cover an entire chapter. As we read, we will notice ways to connect God's work through Nehemiah and his rebuilding project in ancient Jerusalem with the construction project the Holy Spirit has begun in our own hearts and lives today.

As we begin now, we focus on the call of God to Nehemiah, the king's cupbearer. This call placed Nehemiah in an important leadership role, a role critical to the building of the kingdom. As we will see, many stresses and strains threatened to move Nehemiah off the firm stand he had taken, a firm stand upon the Lord, a firm stand of obedience to God's will and for the support and encouragement of God's people as they returned from their seventy-year exile in Babylon.

As this small band of refugees arrived in Jerusalem, they found their homeland reduced to rubble. Their sins and the sins of their parents had brought this disaster upon them. How discouraged and demoralized they must have felt.

But Nehemiah gathered the people to uplift them, to assure them of God's forgiveness, and to take charge of the reconstruction plan. Strengthened by the support and direction they received from God and his servant Nehemiah, the people agreed to start rebuilding.

As the people's leader, Nehemiah connected them to their only secure foundation. Just as the sill plates and tie bolts in a house today sit atop the foundation and secure the building to its foundation, so Nehemiah's prayers, words of pardon, and encouragements linked the people to their gracious, promise-keeping Savior.

How about you? Has God placed a Nehemiah in your life to support you in good times as well as bad? Do you know a Nehemiah who has prayed for you or brought you back to God, encouraging your repentance? Has God placed a Nehemiah in your life to fasten you firmly to the truth that the Lord Jesus forgives your sins and rebuilds your life with two pieces of wood and three nails—the wood and nails of his own cross? What a blessing such an encourager can be! How we need those foundational sills and ties!

I [Nehemiah] . . . told them about the gracious hand of my God upon me.
Nehemiah 2:18

*Prayer suggestion:* Think about whom or what God has used in the past to connect you firmly to your foundation—the Lord Jesus. Pray about that person or event, giving thanks to God!

# Day 23

Foundation Walls
Scriptural Foundation: Nehemiah 3:1–32

The visual in Nehemiah 3 floors me! Did you honestly read every verse? Or did you give in to the temptation to read the first couple of sections and then scan the rest, thinking that it basically restates the same thing while adding all those hard-to-pronounce names besides? Ah, yes, but what a visual! What a lesson!

The people throw themselves into the project. Foundation walls take shape. Gates fly up, then open. Beams, bolts, and bars find their rightful places. The rubble begins to disappear. But in the process something even more astounding happens. The absolute beauty of this construction site lies in how the people work together, side by side. Not only do the stones in the city wall support each other, but so do God's people! Depending on the Bible translation you are reading, the phrase *next to him* appears at least thirteen times.

Mr. So-and-so repaired the next section of the wall while *next to him*, Mr. What's-his-face put doors and bolts and bars in place. One family worked with that guy with the long name and a longer beard to repair the gate, and *next to him* the priest made repairs. One family worked alongside another. Strangers became friends. A father rebuilt a wall and maybe, at the same time, rebuilt a relationship with a son who worked at his side. Is that not an amazing visual?

And it's not all! The first verse of chapter 3 presents a second important point. In it the priests rebuild the Sheep Gate. Then they consecrate it, dedicating it to the Lord. Do we consecrate our work, our days, our decisions, our paperwork, our plans, our meetings, our homes, and our commute time to the Lord? Imagine the joy, the satisfaction, the additional meaning we might find in our work if we did.

Chapter 3 does contain a lot of long, hard-to-pronounce names. We could so easily fall for the temptation to skip over them. But God included them here for a reason. He remembered each individual worker by name. He knew their situations, and he saw how they responded to his forgiveness and grace. He saw how they served him and others in their calling. In grace God even recorded their names in his book to be remembered for all of history.

And your name? God knows it, too—knows you better than you know yourself—and has graciously recorded your name in the Book of Life for all eternity!

Meremoth son of Uriah, the son of Hakkoz, repaired the next section. Next to him Meshullam son of Berekiah, the son of Meshezabel, made repairs, and next to him Zadok son of Baana also made repairs.

Nehemiah 3:4

*Prayer suggestion:* Think about whom or what God has used in the past week to provide the foundational support and strength you need. Pray about that person or event, giving thanks to God!

# Day 24

## Pads, Pilasters, and Piers
Scriptural Foundation: Nehemiah 4:6–23

*Lions and tigers and bears . . . oh my!* In the *Wizard of Oz*, Dorothy, the Tin Man, and the Scarecrow expressed their fear in these words.

*Pads and pilasters and piers . . . oh my!* Maybe that was the cry of fear mumbled by the enemies of Nehemiah and God's people. When Sanballat, Tobiah, and others saw the pads, pilasters, and piers (in essence, the support beams, bolts, and bars) going up on the foundation of Jerusalem's walls, fear led these enemies to voice their opposition. They hated what they saw. They did their best to turn the people's courage into discouragement. While the workers stirred mortar mixture, Sanballat and his crew stirred trouble into the mix.

Soon Nehemiah heard rumors that his crew was growing restless, maybe even ready to walk off the construction site. Satan had successfully used Judah's enemies to panic the workers at the threat that bad guys were about to attack and destroy them. Nehemiah, filled with God's Spirit, came running to the rescue, shoring up the faith and courage of his wall builders:

> Don't be afraid of them. Remember the Lord, who is great and awesome, and fight for your brothers, your sons and your daughters, your wives and your homes.
>
> Nehemiah 4:14

Besides giving God's people encouragement, Nehemiah also gave those people weapons. From then on, they took turns protecting the wall and the friends and family members who were rebuilding it. Those who hauled building materials to the work site did their work with one hand and held a weapon in the other! Armed, yet working. Protecting, yet building.

What tempting voices encourage you to quit today? What words have stirred you into a battle with discouragement? Do not be afraid! Remember the Lord who is great and awesome. Put on his armor, pick up the sword of his Word, and then continue to do what he has called you to do. He will support and steady you.

*Support and safety and salvation . . . oh my!* Jesus, grant it to your servants today!

Don't be afraid of them. Remember the Lord, who is great and awesome.
Nehemiah 4:14

*Prayer suggestion:* Think about whom or what God presently is using as part of your foundational support or strength. Thank him for it.

# Day 25

Pilings
Scriptural Foundation: Nehemiah 5:1–19

Not only did Nehemiah deal with enemies and distractions outside. He also faced Satan, who worked hard to drive wedges between the faithful. Nehemiah 5 details the ways in which some of the people oppressed others when supplies of food and money ran short for many workers and their families.

Still today when money gets tight, anger often picks a fight. Although the people shared the same faith in the same gracious, promise-keeping God, they ended up working against each other instead of working together in unity. Fighting at the wall and fighting outside the wall. Nehemiah called the people together and faced the problem head-on. He placed God's will and Word in front of their eyes. He supported the poor and asked the wealthy to renounce their greed and help those living in poverty. He asked that monies and land be returned to their rightful owners.

Just as pilings provide support for the pads or footings of tall buildings or when soil conditions are poor, so Nehemiah stepped in and became a type of foundation piling for his people. He called each of them to do the same for others. Both sides agreed wholeheartedly! The landowners and the wealthy agreed to return money to and not demand anything else from their brothers in the Lord. Then the story continues:

> *The whole assembly said, "Amen," and praised the LORD.*
> *And the people did as they had promised.*

Nehemiah 5:13

What threatens to steal your peace today? Are bills piling up? Are you feeling buried under a variety of pressures? Deal with the issue head-on. Repent, if necessary. Look the problem right in the eye and don't back down . . . but do kneel down at the cross of Jesus Christ. Seek his wisdom, timing, and help. Pray that God's will becomes clear and that you will have the courage and will to do what is needed.

Then let the body of Christ be the body of Christ. Don't let sinful pride get in the way if the Lord sends you help through a Christian brother or sister. Rejoice that we live together as God's people on the gracious, sure, and solid foundation of Jesus Christ. Then, with the people, worship. Say, "Amen," and praise the Lord!

The whole assembly said, "Amen," and praised the LORD.

Nehemiah 5:13

*Prayer suggestion:* How is God using you as part of someone else's foundational support or strength? Pray for wisdom, discernment, and strength, giving thanks to God for the opportunity to serve!

# Day 26

## Rebar and Wire Mesh
### Scriptural Foundation: Nehemiah 6:1–16

Each foundation component we have considered this week—sill plates, tie bolts, foundation walls, pads, pilasters, piers, and pilings—*support* or connect to something else. But today's components—rebar and wire mesh—*add strength* to foundation walls, footings, grade beams, and concrete slabs.

Who among us wouldn't want more spiritual, mental, and physical strength? You'd think Nehemiah would. Surely he's exhausted by this point in his story—God's story in his life. The opposition from outside of Jerusalem continues. Sanballat begins sending letters full of lies to Nehemiah in the hope of destroying the unity of God's people and intimidating God's servant. But Nehemiah boldly sends this response:

> *"No such things as you say have been done, for you are inventing them out of your own mind." For they all wanted to frighten us, thinking, "Their hands will drop from the work, and it will not be done." But now, O God, strengthen my hands.*

> Nehemiah 6:8–9 ESV

Adding strength to a foundational component isn't the only purpose of rebar and mesh. They also help reduce cracking and settling. Nehemiah didn't crack under the pressure from Satan or his enemies. He didn't settle for less than God's will for this project. God strengthened his hands and the hands of the other faithful workers.

Under God's blessing, the wall was completed—in only fifty-two miraculous days! Nehemiah writes:

> *When all our enemies heard about this, all the surrounding nations were afraid and lost their self-confidence, because they realized that this work had been done with the help of our God.*
>
> Nehemiah 6:16

God is faithful! His foundation stands secure! God uses faithful servants such as Nehemiah . . . and you and me. Thank you, Lord, for Nehemiah and the Nehemiah-like people you have placed in my life! Thank you for all the support and strength you provide for foundational living!

*They realized that this work had been done with the help of our God.*
Nehemiah 6:16

***Prayer suggestion:*** Pray now about challenging spiritual situations you face or anticipate in the near future. Ask God to send you support and strength as you live upon his foundation. And thank God for men, women, and children like Nehemiah who listen and trust in him.

# Days 27–28

## Time for Reflection

### Foundation Components

*Over the next two days, reflect on the message of this hymn. Shape your
prayers around the words as you think back on the meaning of this
week's devotions.*

My hope is built on nothing less
Than Jesus' blood and righteousness;
No merit of my own I claim
But wholly lean on Jesus' name.
On Christ, the solid rock, I stand;
All other ground is sinking sand.

His oath, his covenant, his blood
Sustain me in the raging flood;
When all supports are washed away,
He then is all my hope and stay.
On Christ, the solid rock, I stand;
All other ground is sinking sand.

When he shall come with trumpet sound,
Oh, may I then in him be found,
Clothed in his righteousness alone,
Redeemed to stand before the throne!
On Christ, the solid rock, I stand;
All other ground is sinking sand.

Edward Mote, 1797–1874

# Building for the Future

*The lines of purpose in your lives never grow slack,*
*tightly tied as they are to your future in heaven,*
*kept taut by hope.*

Colossians 1:5 THE MESSAGE

# Day 29

Thankful, Joyful Foundational Living
Scriptural Foundation: Nehemiah 12:27–43; 13:31

L ast week we learned many things from Nehemiah about
building on a solid foundation. Before we move on, our
prophetic friend has one last thing to teach us about
foundational living.

Toward the end of his book, Nehemiah describes the dedication of
the wall of Jerusalem (Nehemiah 12). The gratitude, joy, and
thanksgiving of God's people spilled over the walls and down the
paths leading up to the city on a hill.

Nehemiah asked the leaders of Judah to stand on the top of the
wall. But he didn't stop there. The prophet instructed two huge
choirs and all the instrumentalists to follow the leaders onto the
wall and spread out in each direction:

> *They offered great sacrifices, rejoicing because God had given
> them great joy. The women and children also rejoiced. The
> sound of rejoicing in Jerusalem could be heard far away.*
> Nehemiah 12:43

What confidence Nehemiah placed in his crew and the foundation
upon which they had constructed the wall. He knew it was safe and
secure. Even with both choirs and the leaders all standing on top,
making music, dancing, and stomping their feet in praise, the wall
stood secure.

After describing the time of worship, Nehemiah closes his book with these words:

> *Remember me with favor, O my God.*
>
> Nehemiah 13:31

Nehemiah had carried out God's will to the best of his ability. He had sought the face of the Lord. He made certain the people's lives, as well as their wall, were built on the right, sure, and firm foundation. He had placed his life in God's hands, humbled and honored that God used him.

But Nehemiah is not the hero of this story! The Lord is the true hero. He chose, forgave, and empowered Nehemiah. The Lord gave the people a heart for work and protected them from their enemies. So, too, in our lives the Lord is the true hero. He chooses, forgives, empowers, heartens, and protects. Praise him!

*Remember me with favor, O my God.*

Nehemiah 13:31

***Prayer suggestion:*** Praise and thank God over and over again. Sing it, play it, speak it aloud! Let loose! It's a regular part of life built upon the foundation of Jesus Christ.

# Day 30

The Living Cornerstone and Living Stones
Scriptural Foundation: 1 Peter 2:4–8

Often only decorative today, the cornerstone in ancient times served as the foundational rock of most buildings. Set on a corner of the foundation before any other stone was added, the cornerstone became the model for every other stone placed around and upon it. If the size and quality of this cornerstone was not right, the entire building would list and possibly even collapse. The cornerstone—and the one who chose it—held very responsible positions!

The apostle Peter calls Jesus the believer's cornerstone. He describes this cornerstone as handpicked, chosen, and precious. The apostle also describes Jesus Christ as the living cornerstone (1 Peter 2:4–8). The world rejected Jesus, but God chose him and declared him precious and perfect, the perfect sacrifice for our redemption and salvation.

And there's more! Jesus, the living cornerstone, has also chosen us to be living stones, built upon him to form the temple in which God himself dwells, the church. Christ's grace and righteousness bring each of us into perfect alignment with himself and God's holy will.

In a quarry, stones survive a variety of experiences that eventually determine their shape and the purposes for which they can serve best in a building. They may be cut, chiseled, or hammered. This process creates their character and makes them fit perfectly into their position in the building. The same is true for us.

With his kingdom-building plan always in mind, our architect, foundation, and cornerstone—Christ Jesus—handpicks us to fit in just the right place in his church. He washes us clean with his forgiveness, chisels away our imperfections, and sets us in place, firmly upon himself—our foundation and foundational cornerstone.

> *As you come to him, a living stone rejected by men but in the sight of God chosen and precious, you yourselves like living stones are being built up as a spiritual house, to be a holy priesthood, to offer spiritual sacrifices acceptable to God through Jesus Christ.*

1 Peter 2:4–5 ESV

*The one who trusts in him will never be put to shame.*

1 Peter 2:6

***Prayer suggestion:*** Jesus, my cornerstone, I'm both humbled and overjoyed that you chose me to stand beside you as a living stone in your house. Shape and purify me to worthiness in your sight, by your cross alone. Your love overwhelms me, Jesus. Amen.

# Day 31

Living Stones
Scriptural Foundation: 1 Peter 2:4–8

In his teaching series "That the World May Know," Ray Vander Laan shares a wonderful tradition from the culture of the Middle East. When something significant of a religious nature happens, you take a stone and stand it up on that spot so that whoever sees the stone can ask, "What happened here?" That question then gives the person who sets up the monument an opportunity to tell the questioner what God did on that exact spot.

When God brought his people safely through the Jordan River and into the Promised Land, he had them stand twelve stones (representing the twelve families or tribes of Israel) in the river. Then the Lord said:

> *In the future, when your children ask you, "What do these stones mean?" tell them that the flow of the Jordan was cut off before the ark of the covenant of the LORD. When it crossed the Jordan, the waters of the Jordan were cut off. These stones are to be a memorial to the people of Israel forever.*
>
> Joshua 4:6–7

What a blessing it would be if our lives could serve this same function! What a blessing if people around us would notice the way we respond to problems, the way we act in love, the way we make decisions, the way we raise our children, and would be moved to ask, "What happened here?" What a blessing if we could say, "Let me tell you what God did."

In our homes, our schools, our neighborhoods, our churches, our walking trails, in our courthouses, and even in our prisons—

wherever God's people are found—we can witness in word and actions to God, who acts in our lives in specific and powerful ways.

By grace, we're living stones! By grace, we're chosen and perfectly set on the cornerstone and foundation of Jesus Christ. By God's grace, may others see our actions and honor our Father in heaven.

*You also, like living stones, are being built into a spiritual house to be a holy priesthood, offering spiritual sacrifices acceptable to God through Jesus Christ.*

1 Peter 2:5

*Prayer suggestion:* Lord Jesus, my living cornerstone, I pray that my life will stand as a monument to your honor always. In times of temptation and blessing, prosperity and persecution, may I shout your faithfulness to a world filled with sin and hopelessness. May I proclaim that you are a living God who truly does miraculous things. In your own precious name, Lord Jesus. Amen.

# Day 32

## Expansion Plans
### Scriptural Foundation: John 14:1–6

Most of us don't spend a lot of time thinking about our heavenly home. We focus instead on the here and now. We know—perhaps from memory—each detail of what our home or apartment on earth looks like, but we can't really begin to visualize our home in heaven.

In John 14:1–6, the disciples let it be known that Jesus' future plans for them, plans that included taking them home to himself in heaven, left them scratching their heads. So to remove some of the mystery, the Lord gave them a glimpse of his plans to build and expand that heavenly home. Jesus told his disciples:

> In my Father's house are many rooms. If it were not so, would I have told you that I go to prepare a place for you? And if I go and prepare a place for you, I will come again and will take you to myself, that where I am you may be also.
>
> John 14:2–3 ESV

Then Jesus warned the disciples that only one path leads to heaven, and he himself is that path. Jesus said:

> I am the way, and the truth, and the life. No one comes to the Father except through me.
>
> John 14:6 ESV

What did the disciples visualize when they heard these words? Most likely they pictured what happened in their day when the bridegroom came to take his fiancée home to live permanently with him. In that culture, the bridegroom helped build a room onto his family's house before the wedding took place. The young couple would then move into the new wing of the family home. As other sons and daughters married, the home grew. Eventually, the father's house had many rooms—all built for the children, all built directly onto the ancestral home.

Knowing this custom, now marvel over God's blueprint for heaven's expansion! Praise him for the part you play in it as you tell others about our Savior, his plan of salvation, and his forgiving grace. The marriage feast lies just around the corner. By grace, through faith in Jesus, we'll enjoy forever the addition Jesus has designed and built especially for us! Whom will you be bringing along with you?

*If I go and prepare a place for you, I will come again and will take you to myself, that where I am you may be also.*

John 14:3 ESV

*Prayer suggestion:* Create within me, Holy Spirit, a deep awe and appreciation for your gift of heaven. Stir within me the zeal to share your news of salvation in the cross of Jesus, my Savior, in whose name I pray. Amen.

# Day 33

The Red Prints on the Blueprints
Scriptural Foundation: Revelation 1:4–6

Over the past five weeks we've explored some fundamental and eternal truths from Scripture about what it means to live on the foundation and aligned with the cornerstone, Jesus Christ. We've surveyed God's blueprints for living and visited two key construction sites—that on which Nehemiah served as the foreman and that on which our own lives are being built.

Before we leave these sites, pause one last time to study God's blueprint for your life. While you do, notice one last important thing. Do you now see the red prints that appear across the blueprints for your life? They are not a mistake. Nor were they added as an afterthought. These bloody fingerprints signify your Savior's close, personal concern about every detail of your life.

As those details unfold day by day, you will seldom know for certain what will happen next, what experiences—wonderful or devastating—you might encounter. One thing is certain, however. Nothing will happen in your life that has not first passed through the hands of your Savior. Those hands still bear the nail scars by which he bought your forgiveness. Thus, there can be no doubt: his hands are hands of love. His bloody sacrifice on the cross has covered your sins, every one of them. Yes, you read that correctly—*every* sin!

As your life's events unfold, you can trust that Jesus stands beside you, upholding you each and every second. And because his blood covers the blueprints of your life, you can be sure that heaven's door stands open, ready for your arrival one day. There you will find yourself welcomed into a new, eternal home made ready for you by Jesus, your Savior, just as he has promised:

> *Grace to you and peace from Him who is and who was and who is to come, and from the seven Spirits who are before His throne, and from Jesus Christ, the faithful witness, the firstborn from the dead, and the ruler over the kings of the earth. To Him who loved us and washed us from our sins in His own blood, and has made us kings and priests to His God and Father, to Him be glory and dominion forever and ever. Amen.*

Revelation 1:4–6 NKJV

Abundant and heavenly blessings on your life lived on the foundation of Jesus Christ!

*To Him be glory and dominion forever and ever. Amen.*

Revelation 1:6 NKJV

***Prayer suggestion:*** To him who loved us and washed us from our sins in his own blood and has made us kings and priests to his God and Father, to you, Jesus, be glory and dominion forever and ever. Amen!

# Days 34–35

## Time for Reflection

### Building for the Future

*Over the next two days, reflect on the message of this hymn. Shape your prayers around the words as you think back on the meaning of this week's devotions.*

Abide with us, our Savior,
Nor let your mercy cease;
From Satan's might defend us,
And give our hearts your peace.

Abide with us, our Helper,
Sustain us by your Word;
Let us and all your people
To living faith be stirred.

Abide as our protector
Among us, Lord, our strength;
Let world and wily Satan
Be overcome at length.

Abide among us always,
O Lord, our faithful friend,
And take us to your mansions
When time and world shall end.

Joshua Stegmann, 1588–1632;
tr. August Crull

You are God's house.
Using the gift God gave me
as a good architect,
I designed blueprints;
Apollos is putting up the walls.
Let each carpenter who comes on the job
take care to build on the foundation!
Remember, there is only one foundation,
the one already laid:
Jesus Christ.

1 Corinthians 3:9–11 THE MESSAGE

Then I said to them,
"You see the trouble we are in. . . .
Come, let us rebuild the wall of Jerusalem,
and we will no longer be in disgrace."
I also told them about the gracious hand
of my God upon me
and what the king had said to me.

*They replied, "Let us start rebuilding."*
*So they began this good work.*

Nehemiah 2:17–18

*Let the Word of Christ—the Message—*
*have the run of the house.*
*Give it plenty of room in your lives.*

Colossians 3:16 THE MESSAGE

*My hope is built on nothing less*
*Than Jesus' blood and*
*righteousness;*
*No merit of my own I claim*
*But wholly lean on Jesus' name.*
*On Christ, the solid rock, I stand;*
*All other ground is sinking sand.*

Edward Mote, 1797–1874